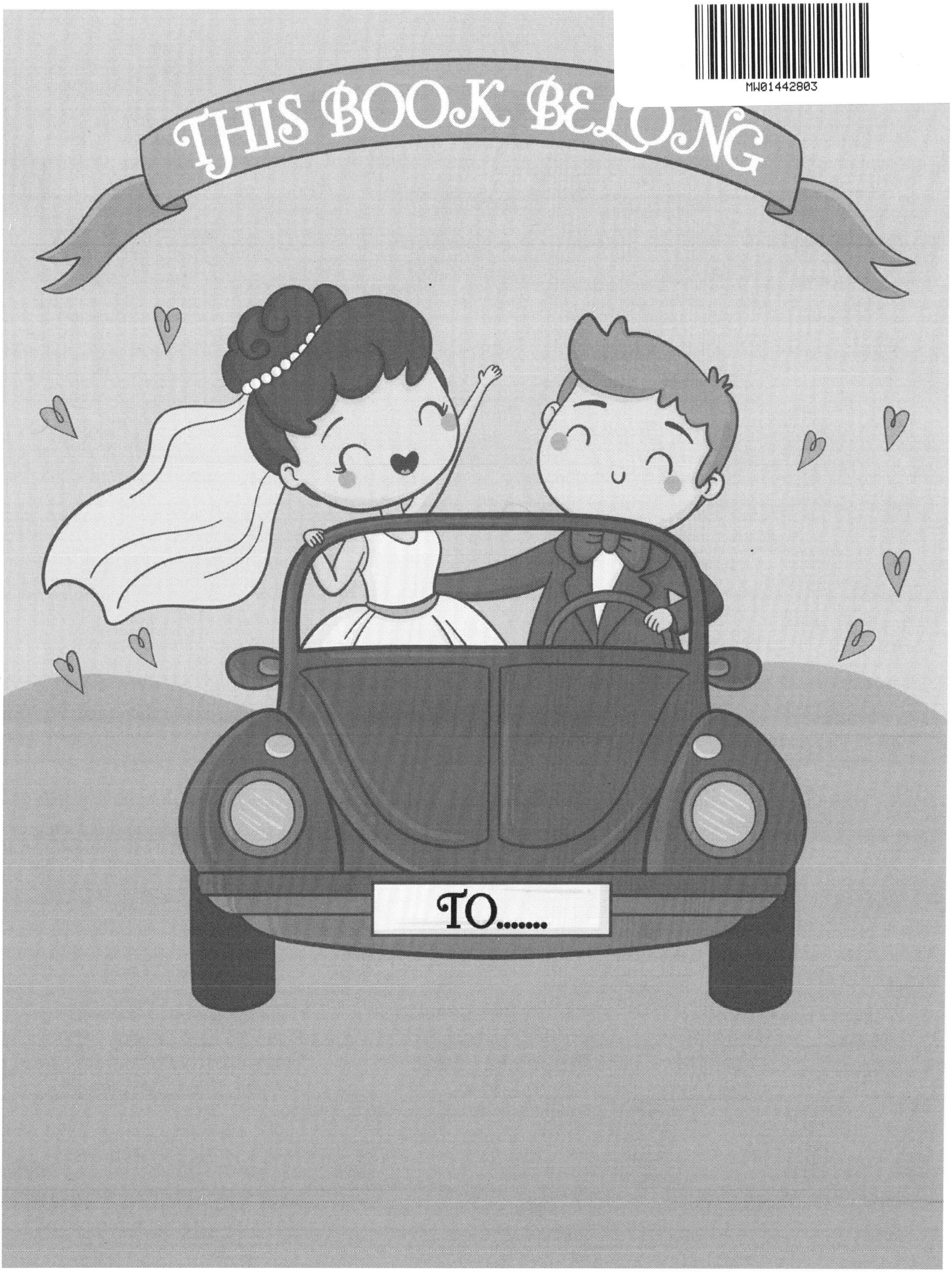
THIS BOOK BELONG
TO.......

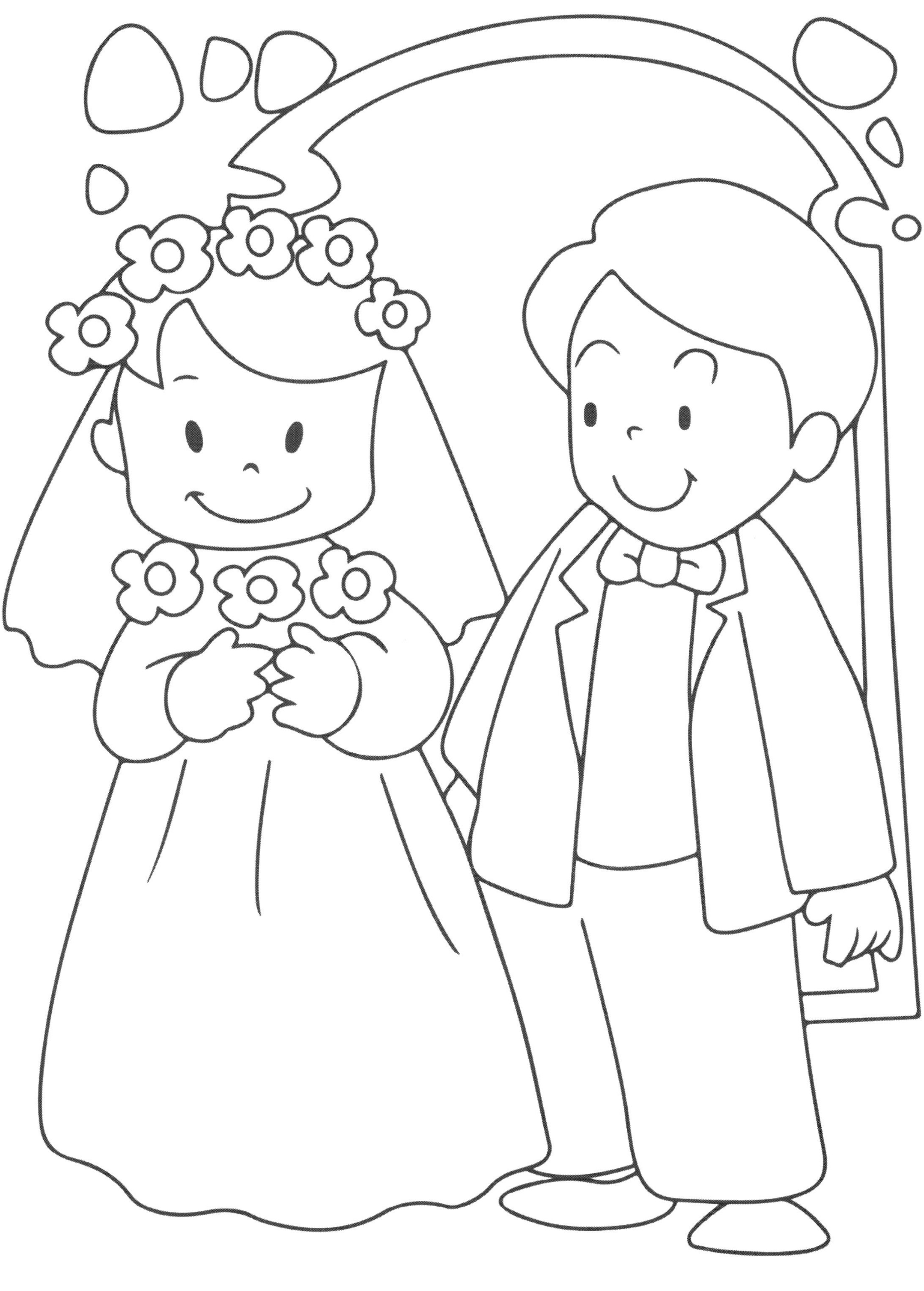

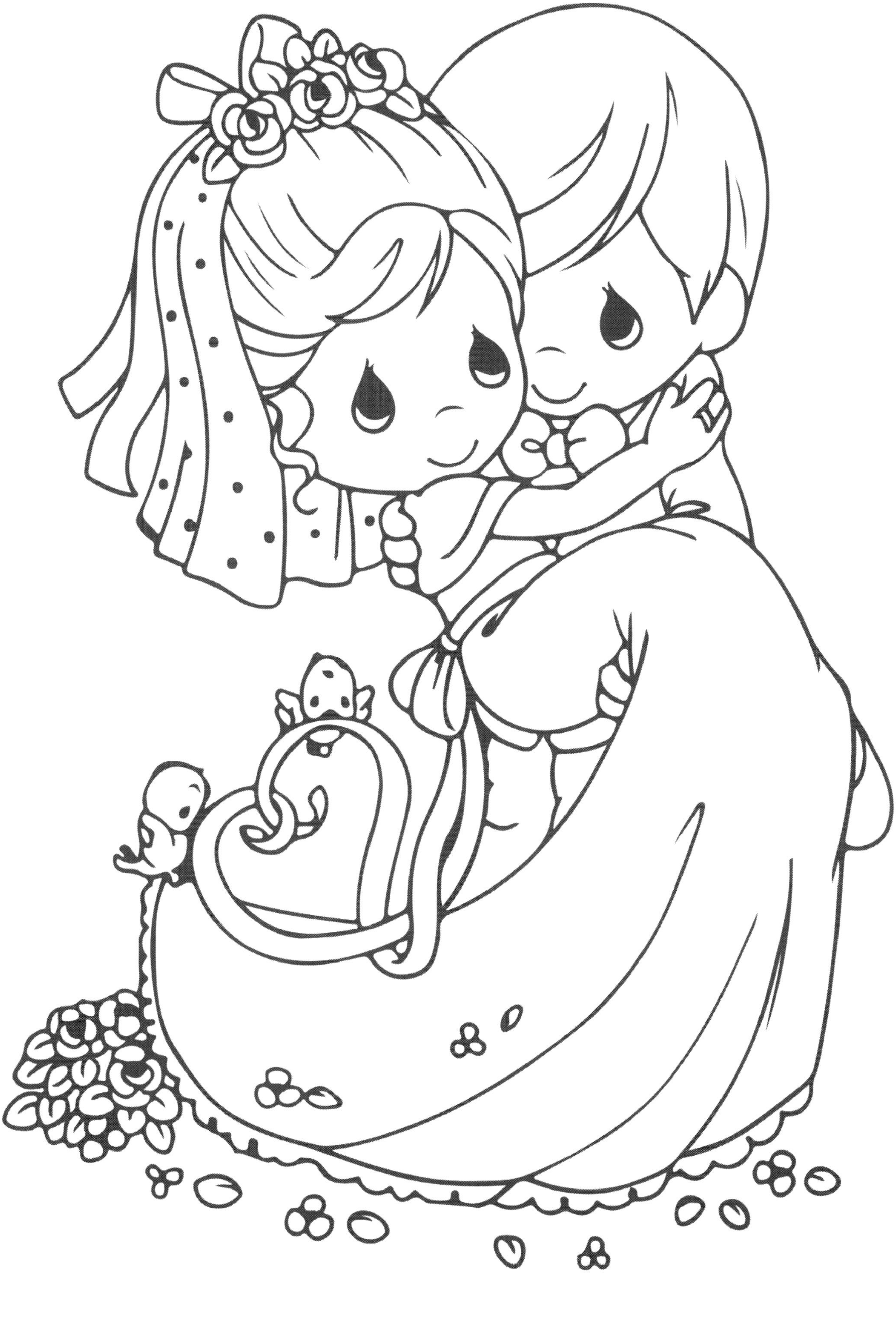

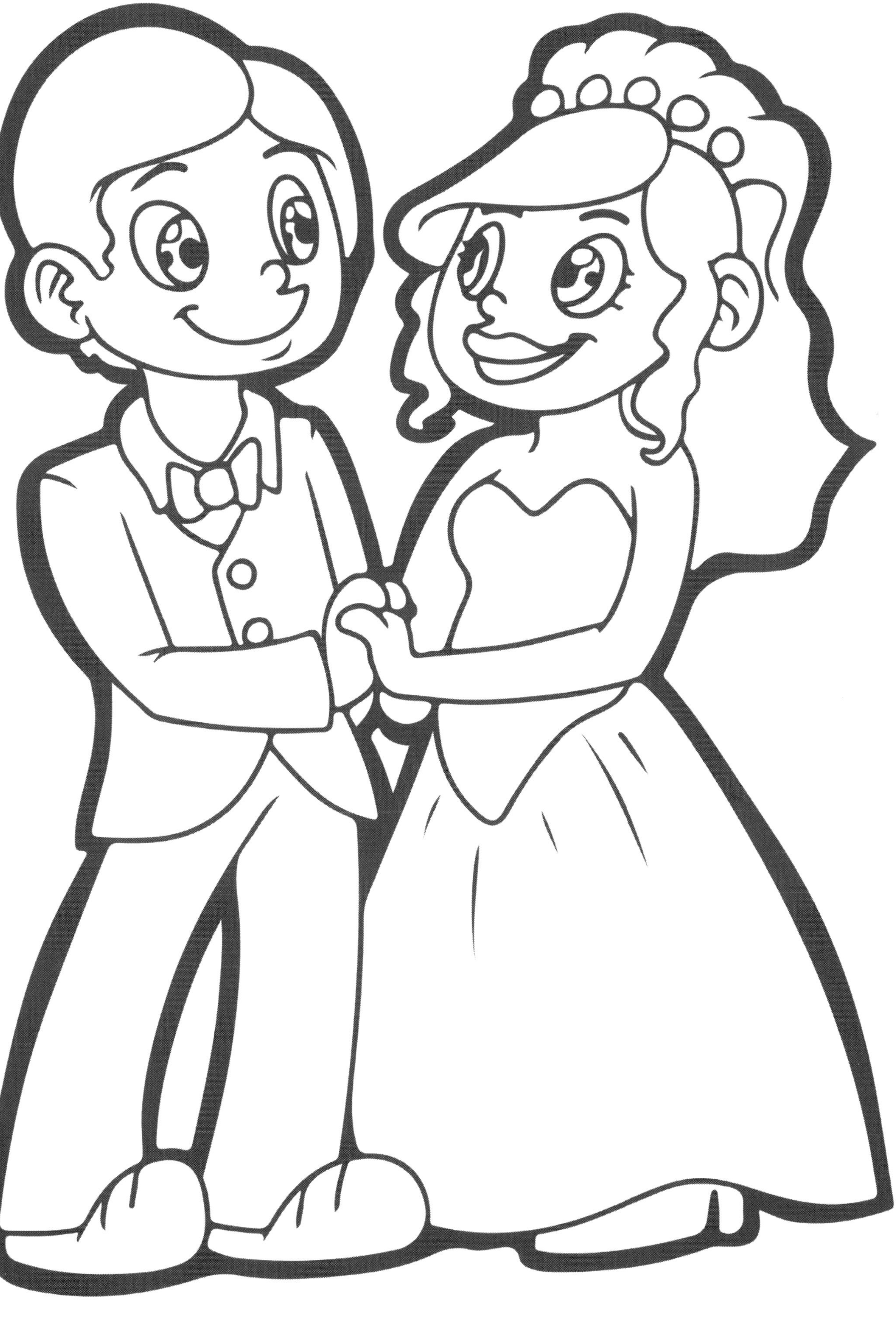

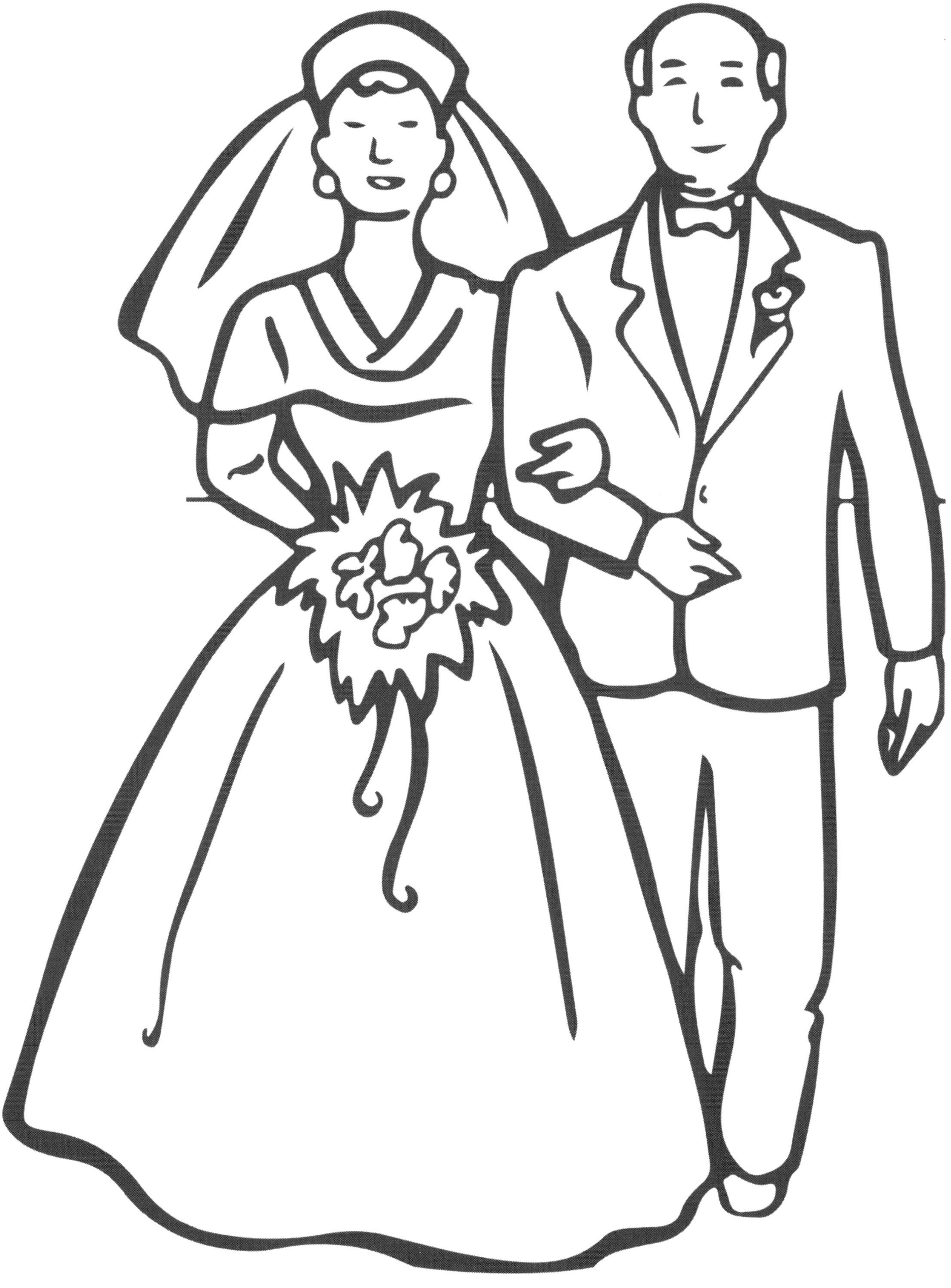

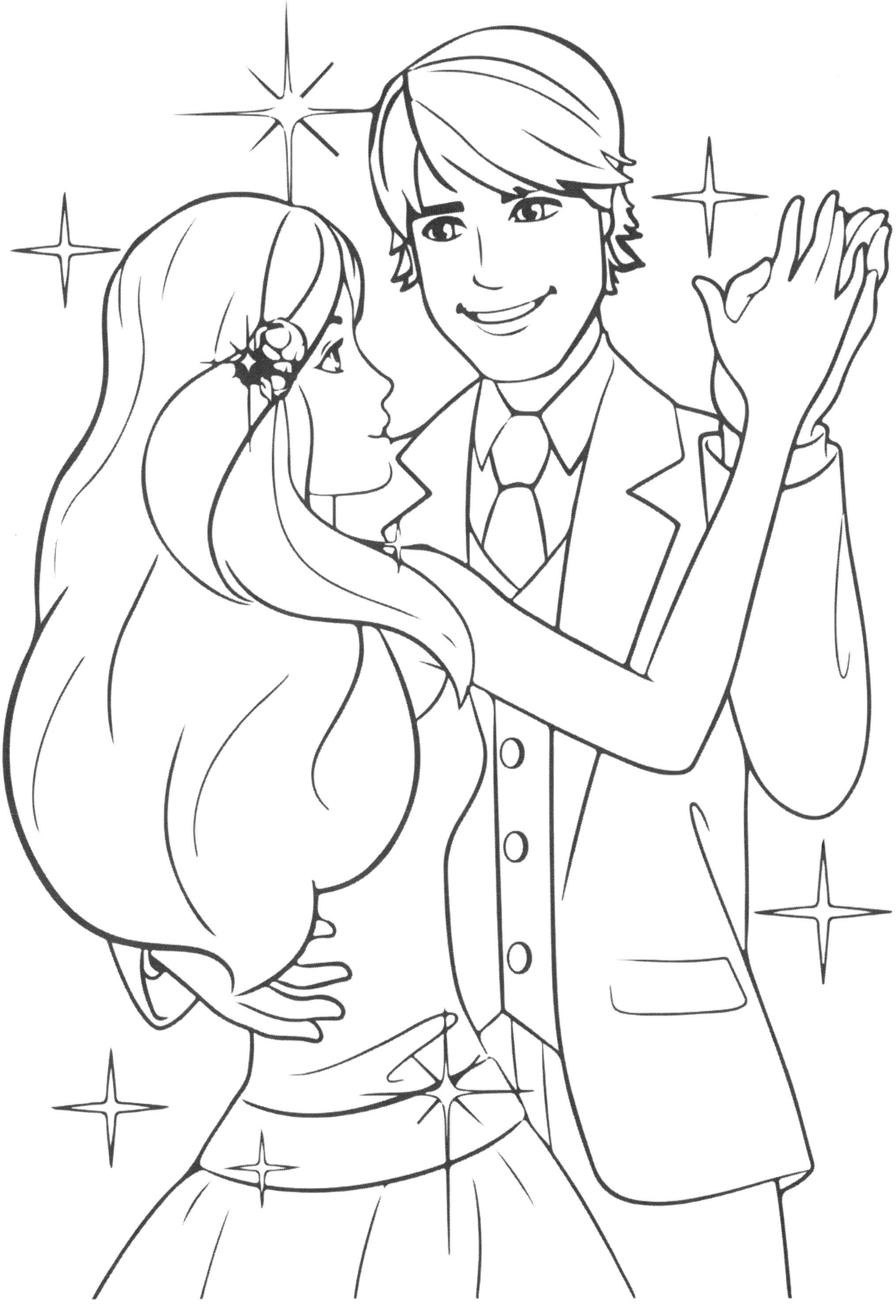

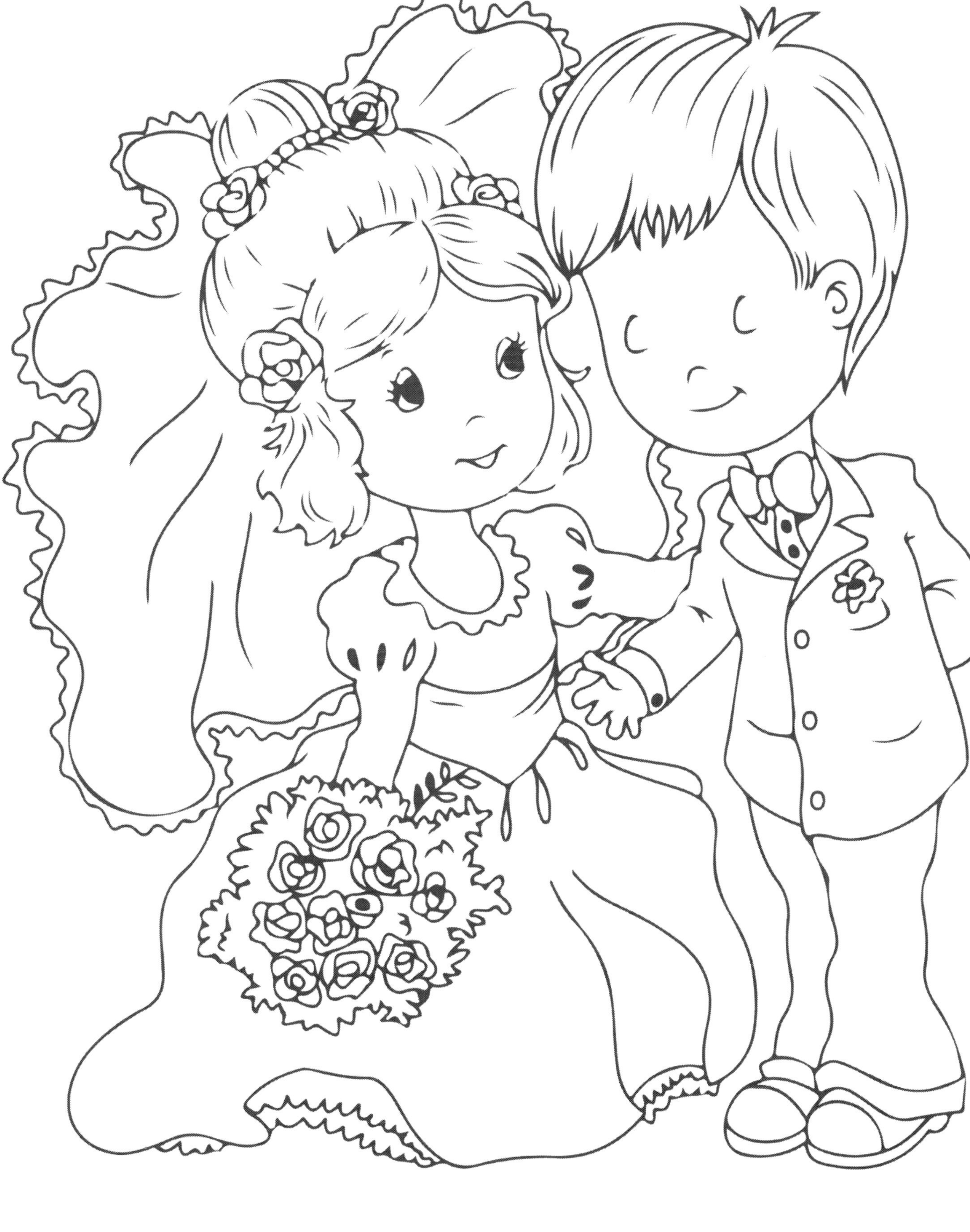

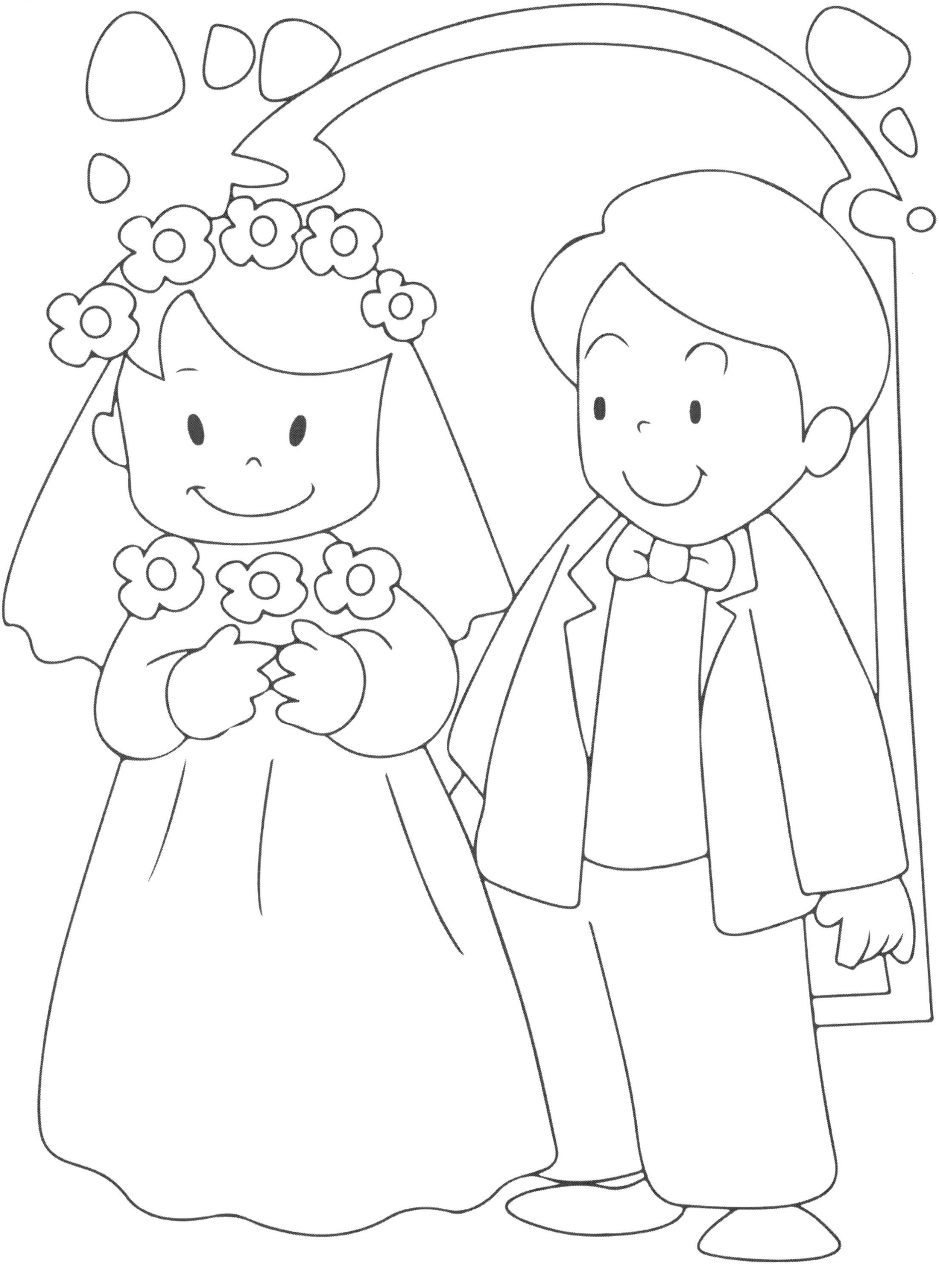

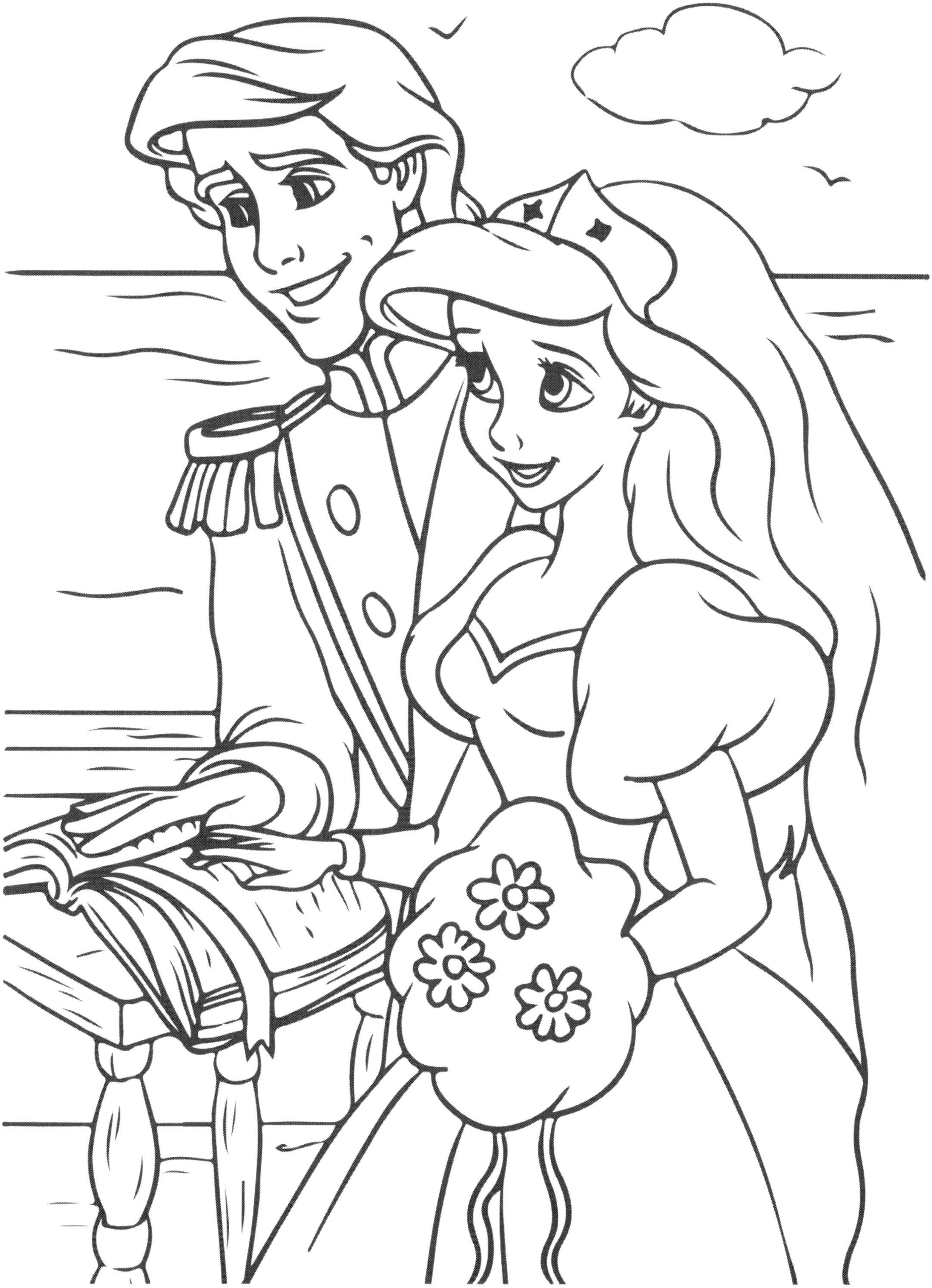

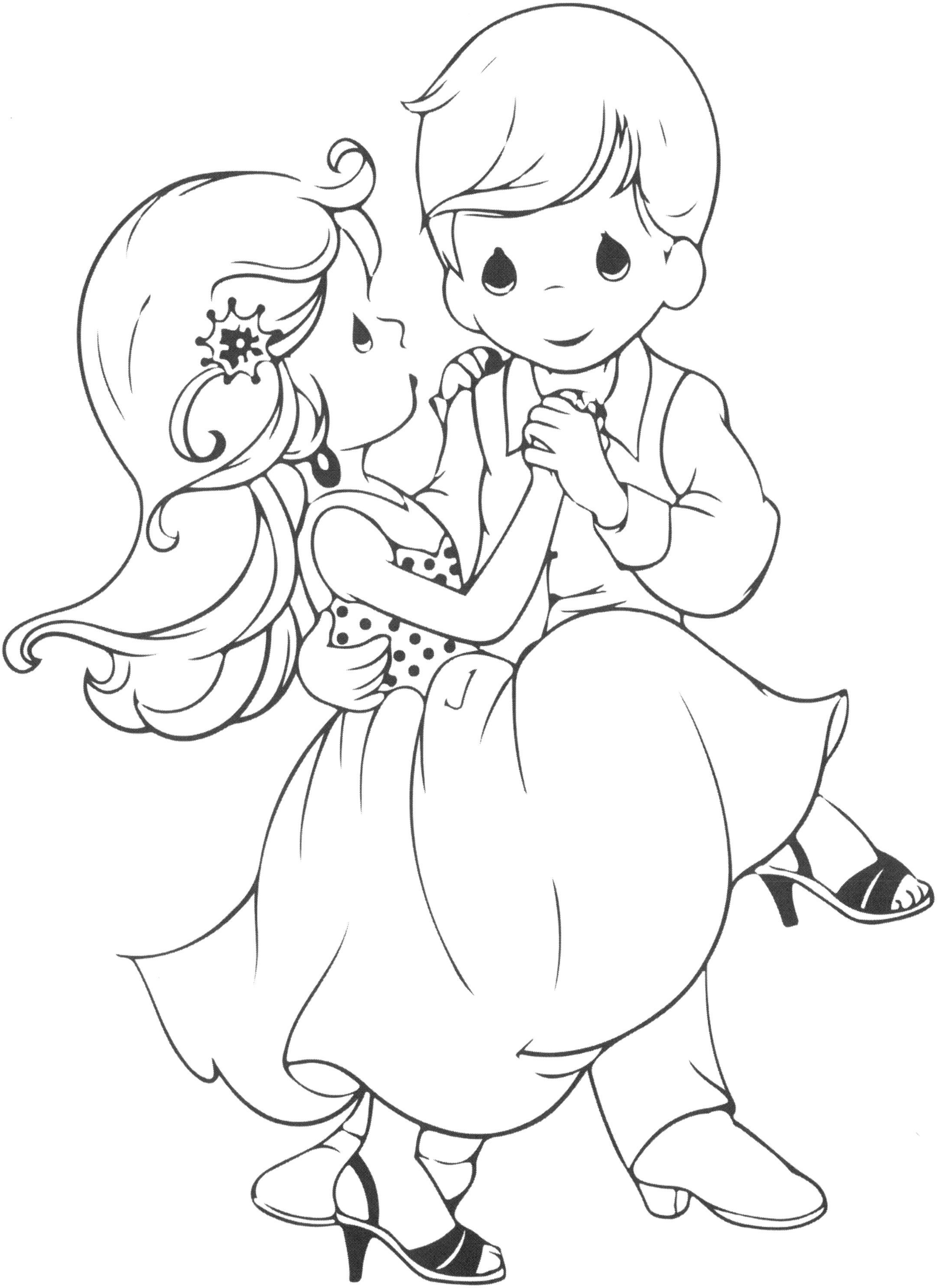

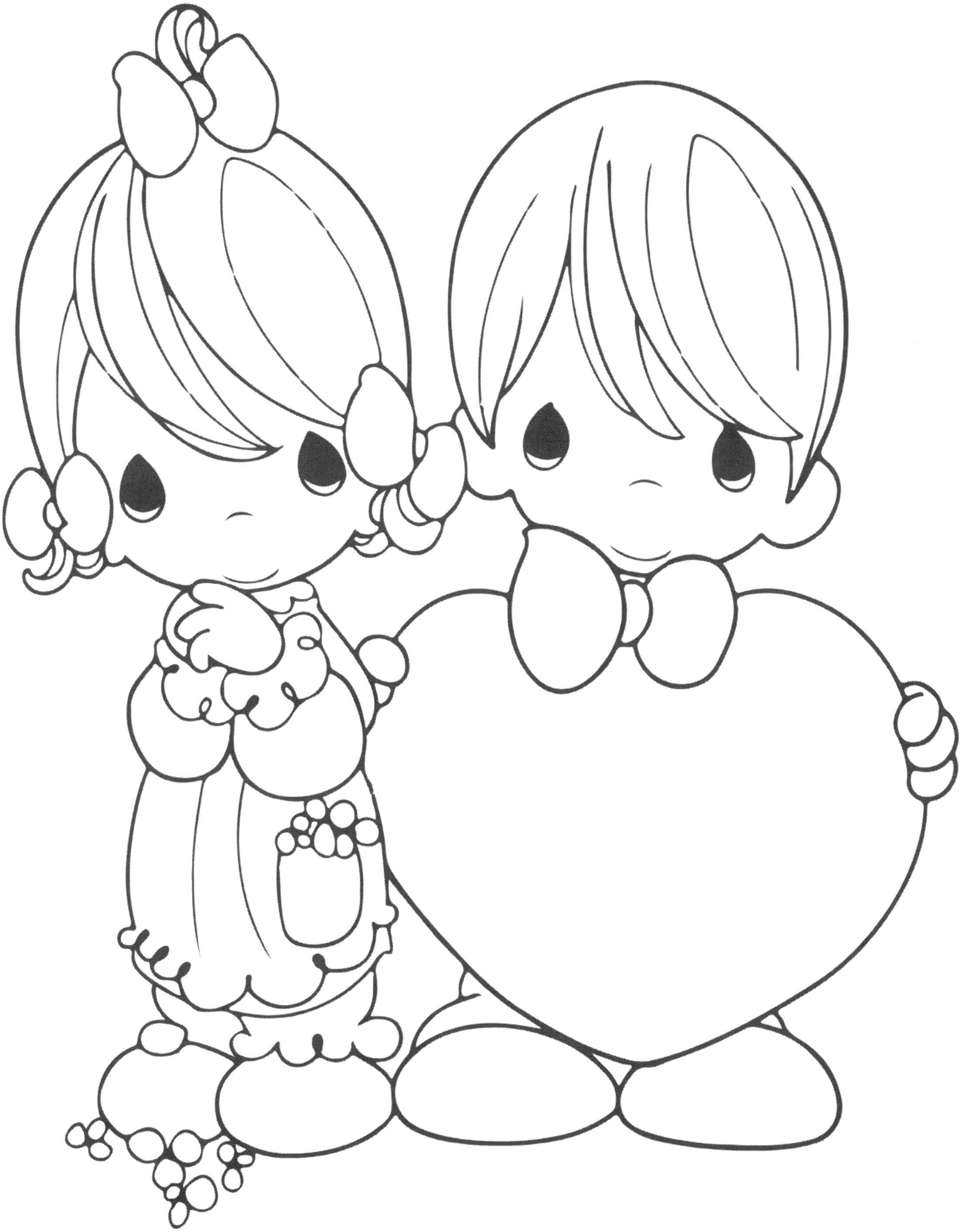

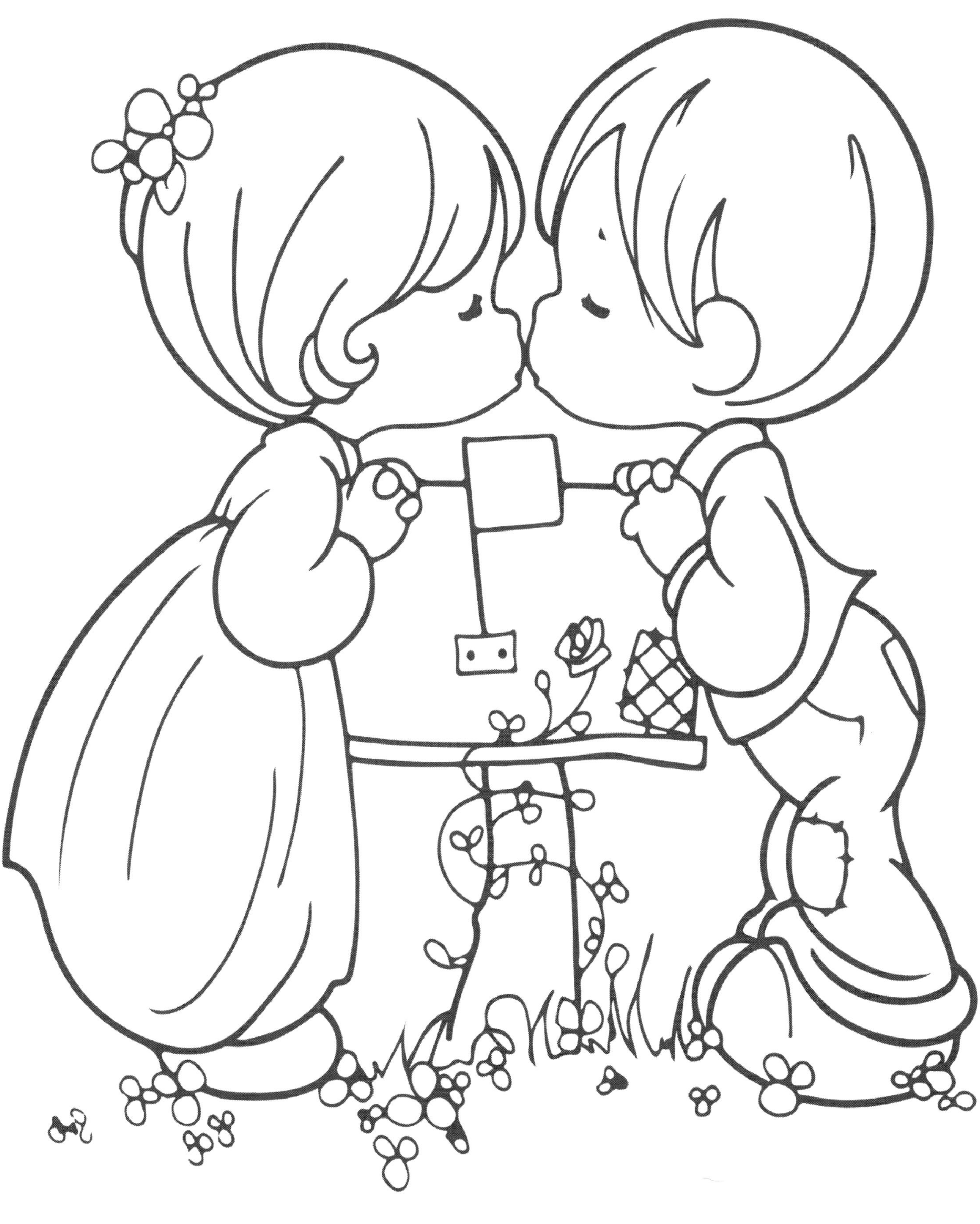

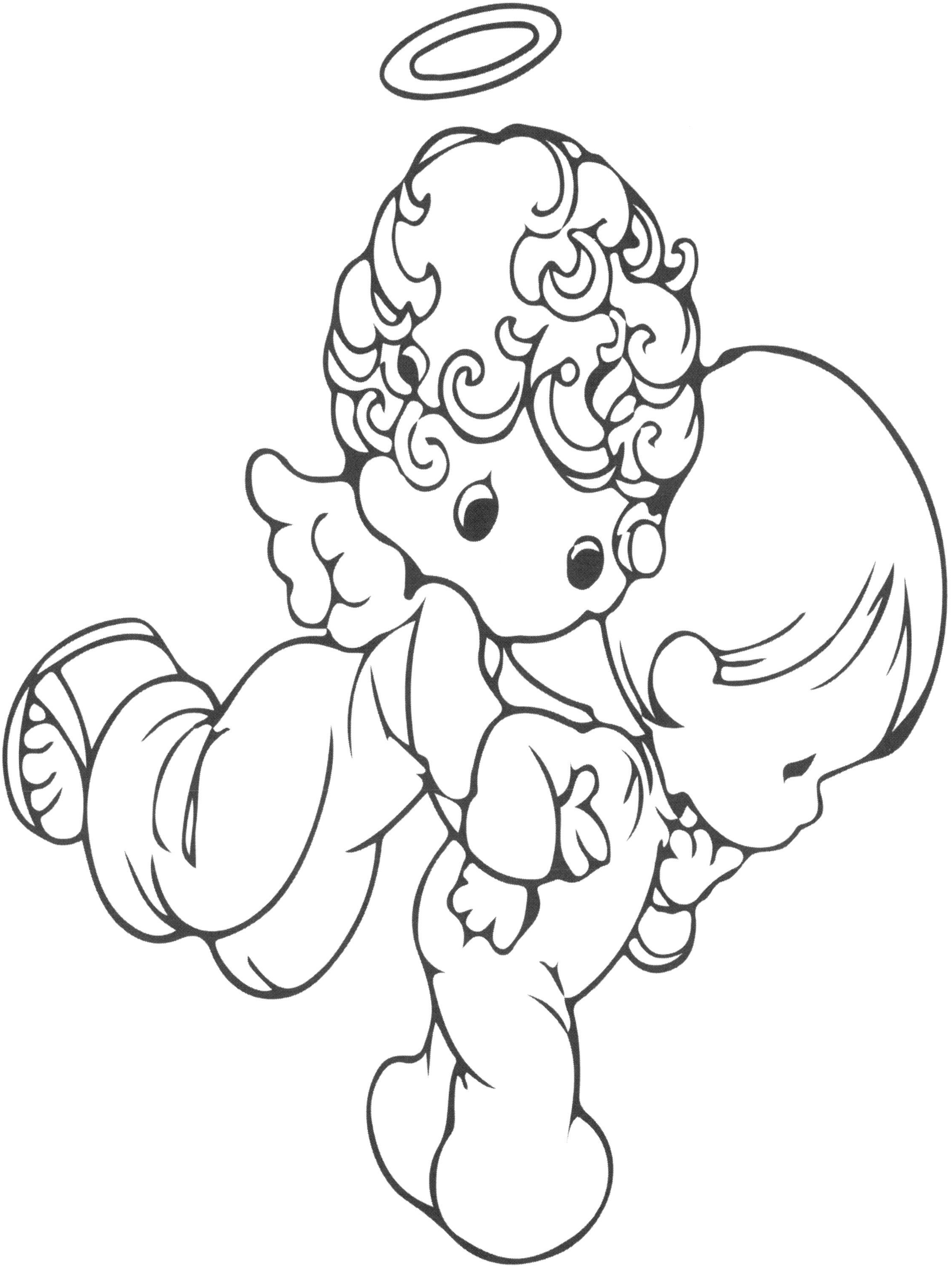

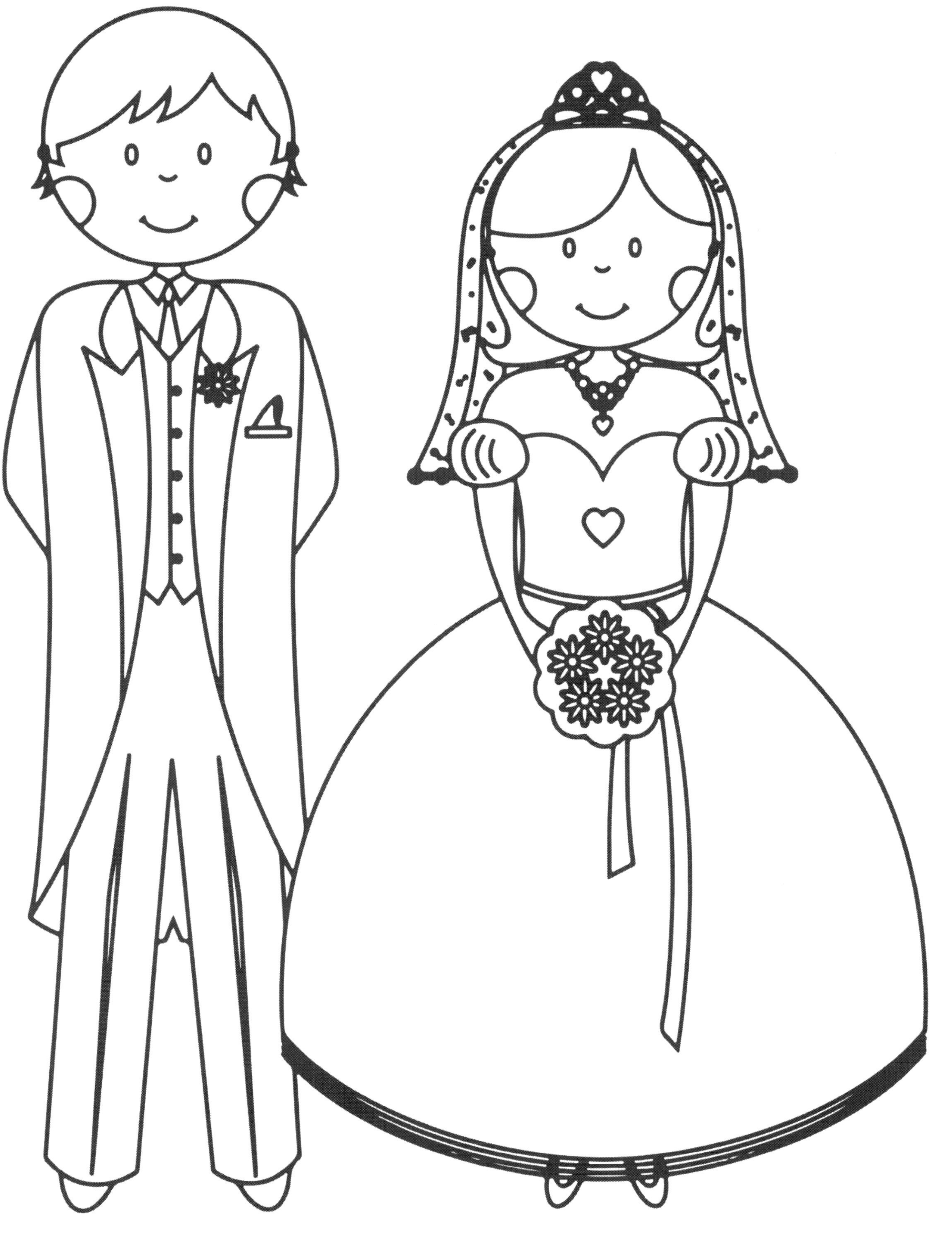

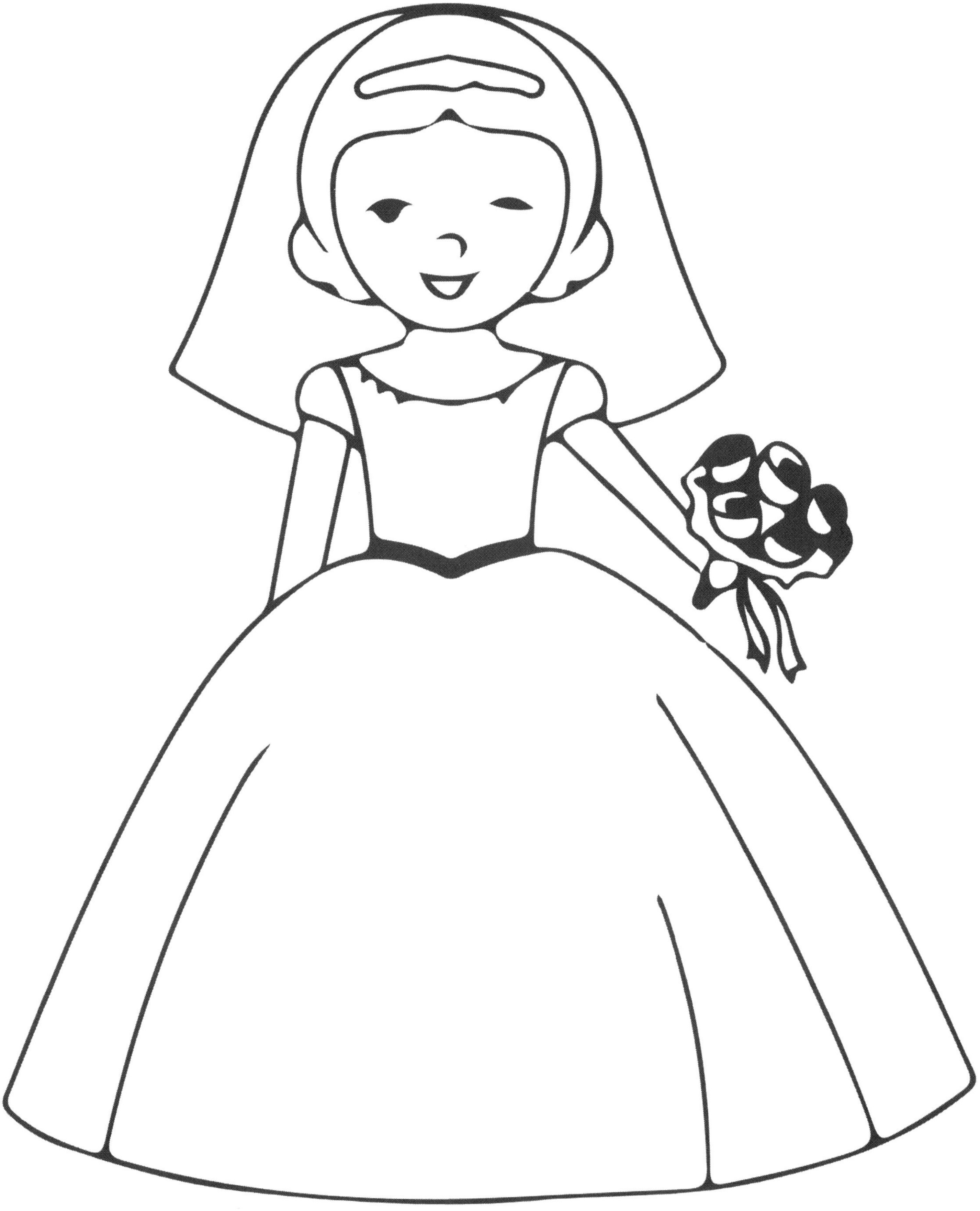

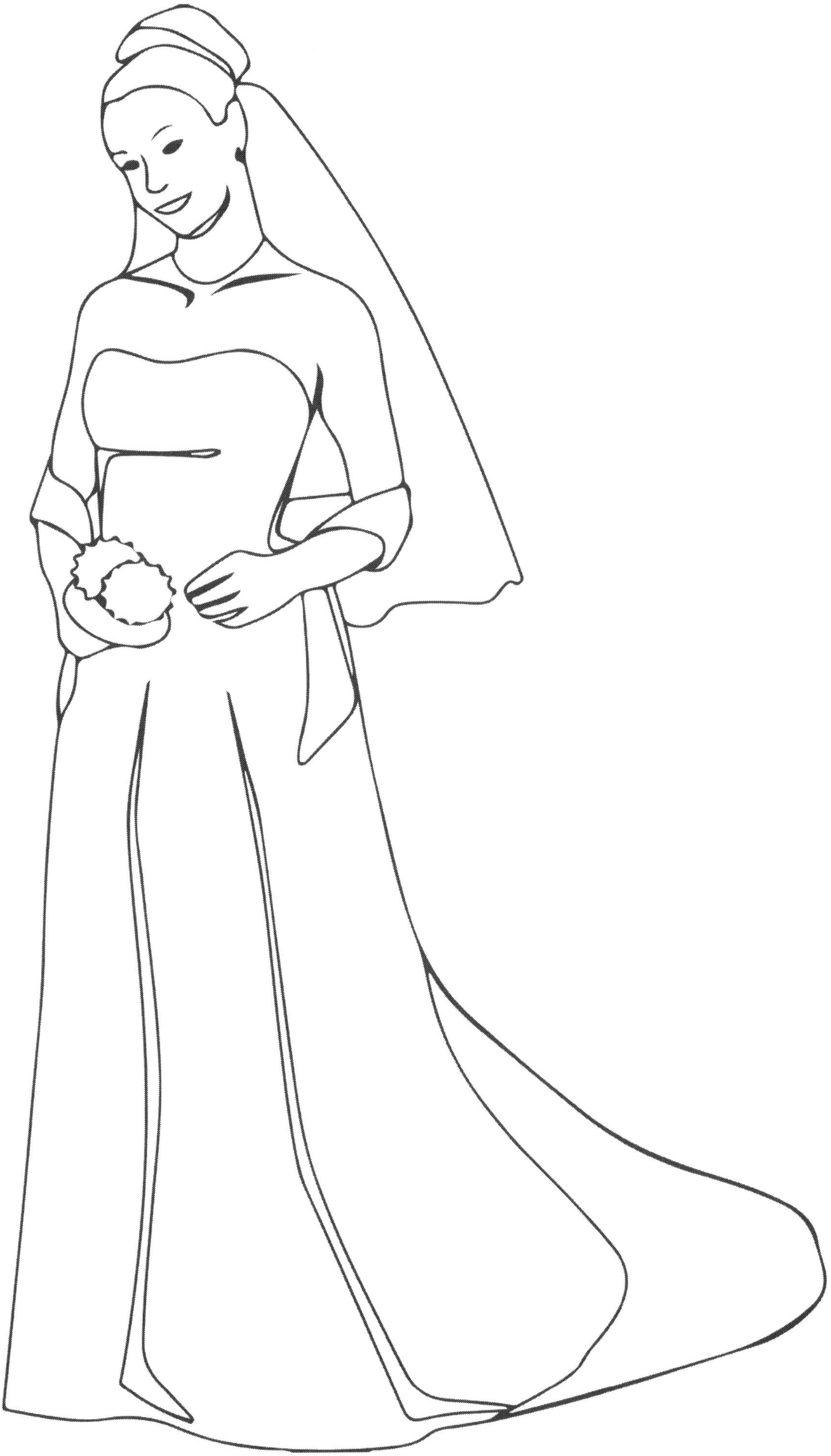

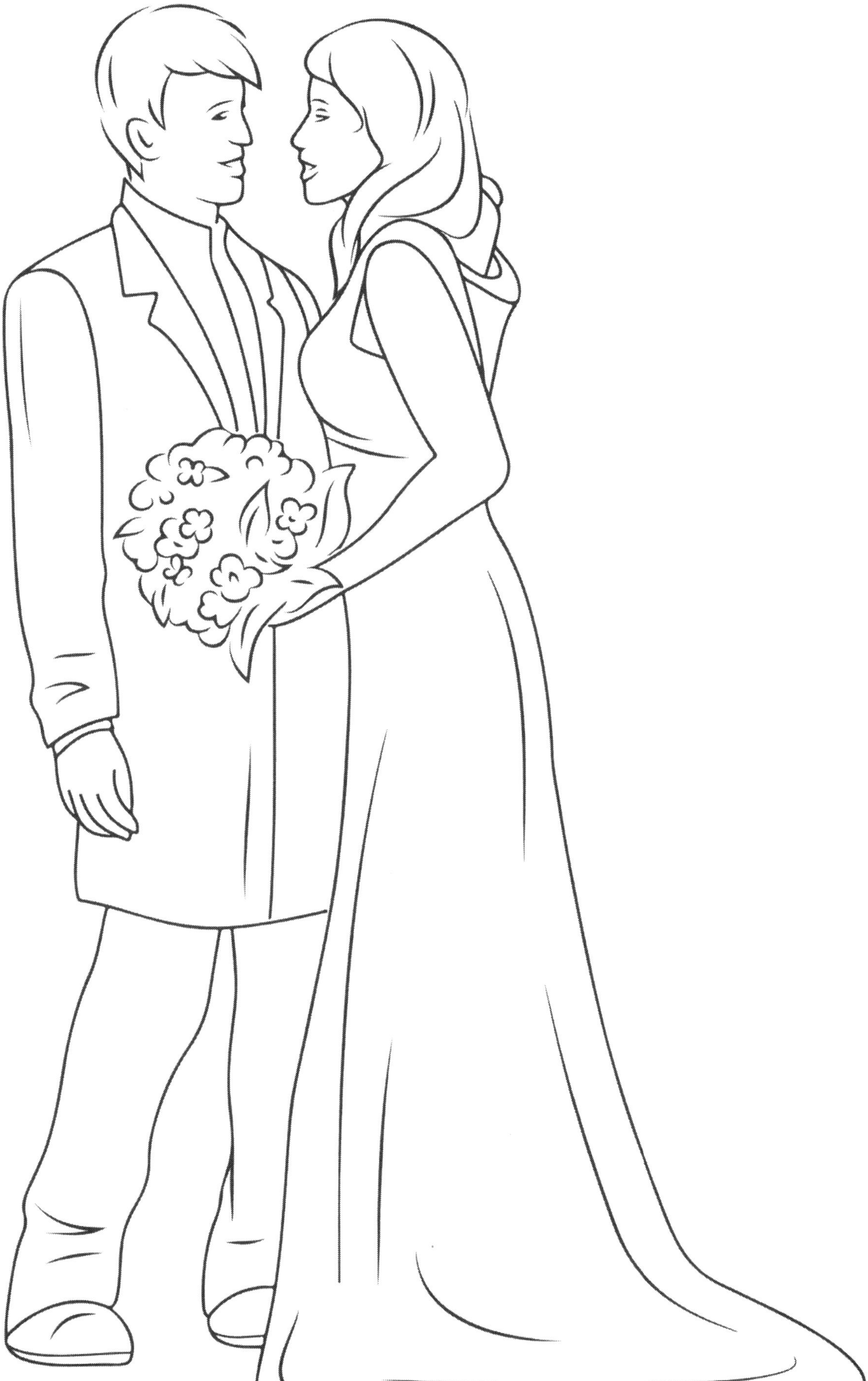

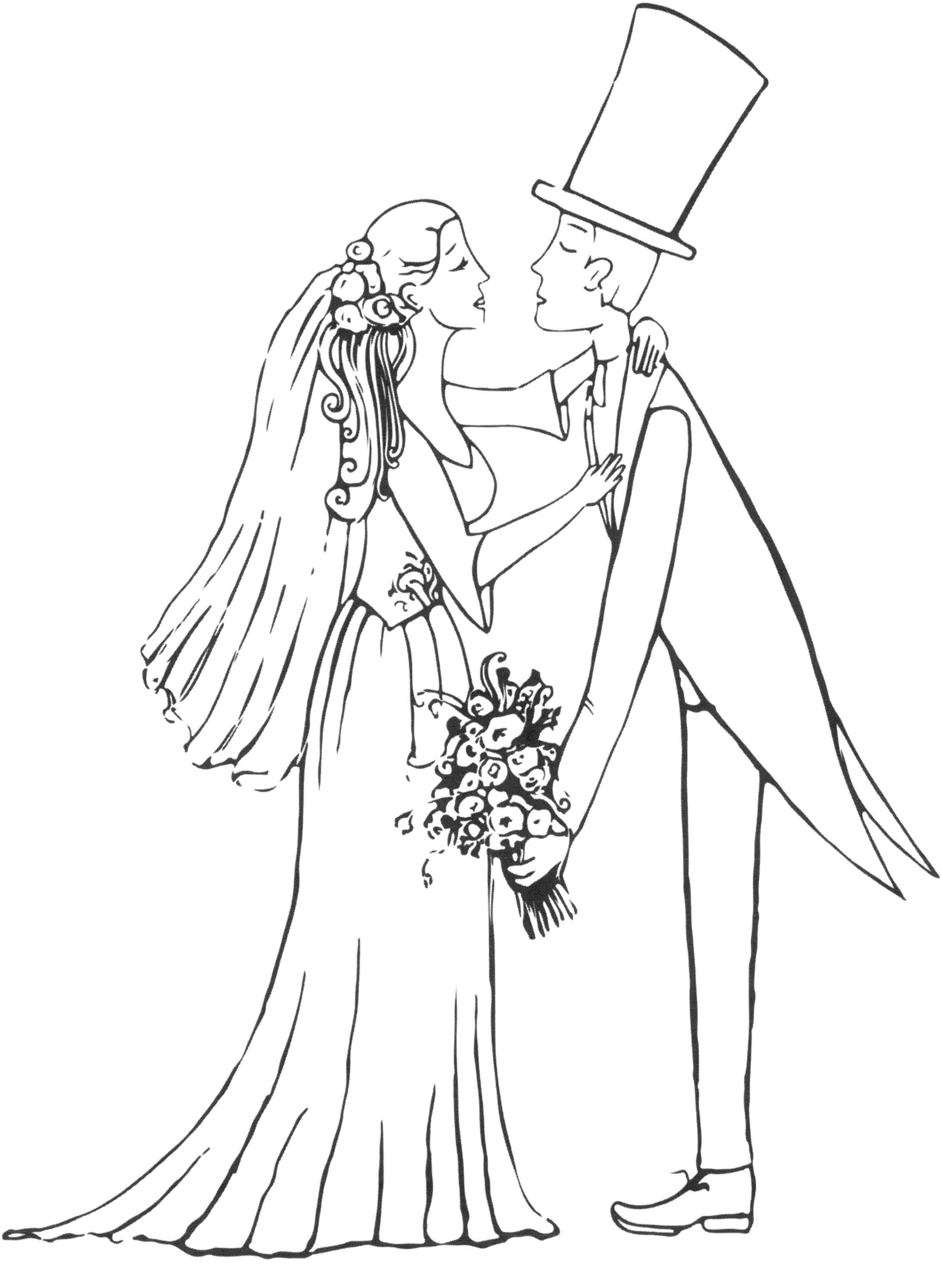

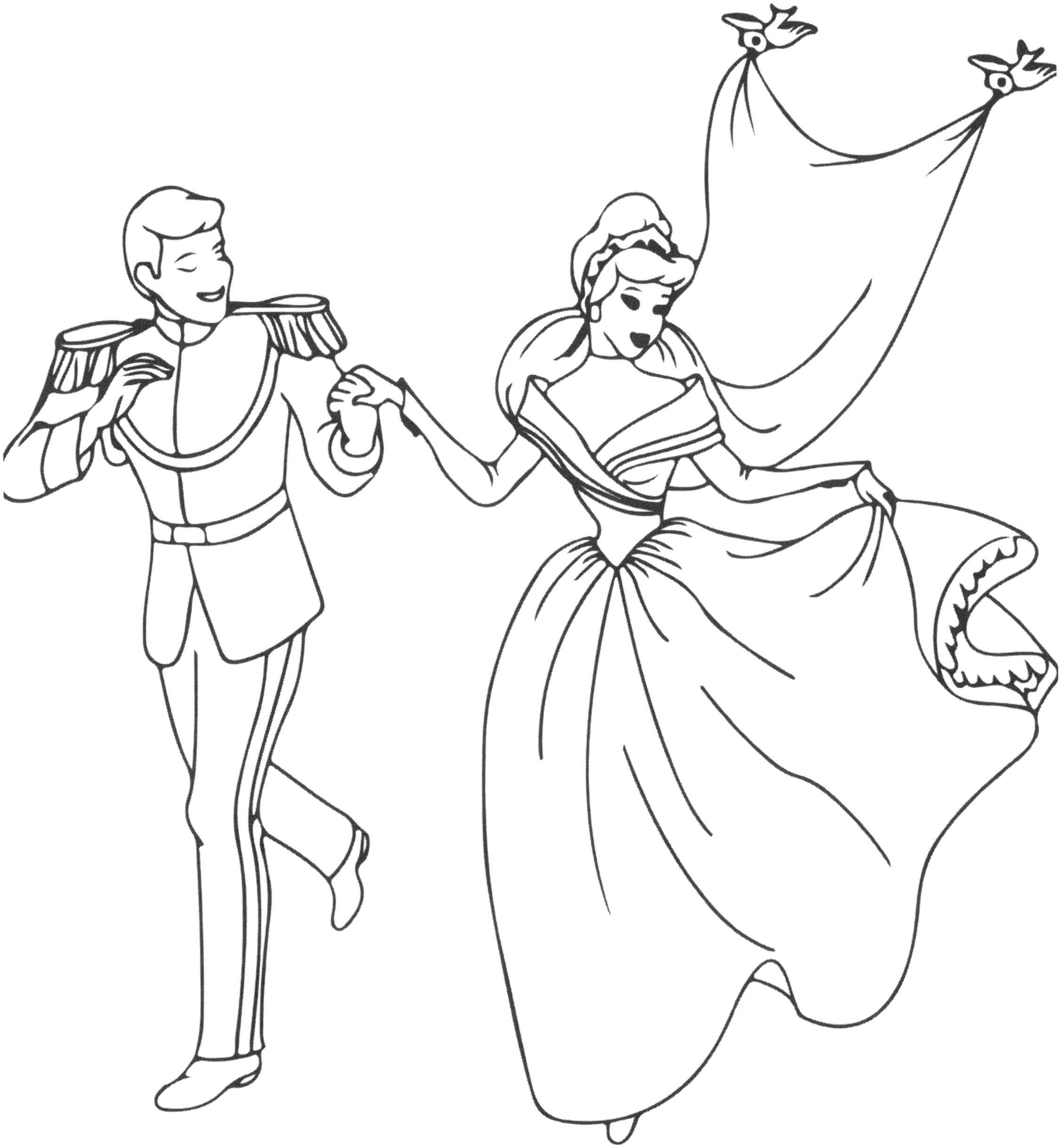

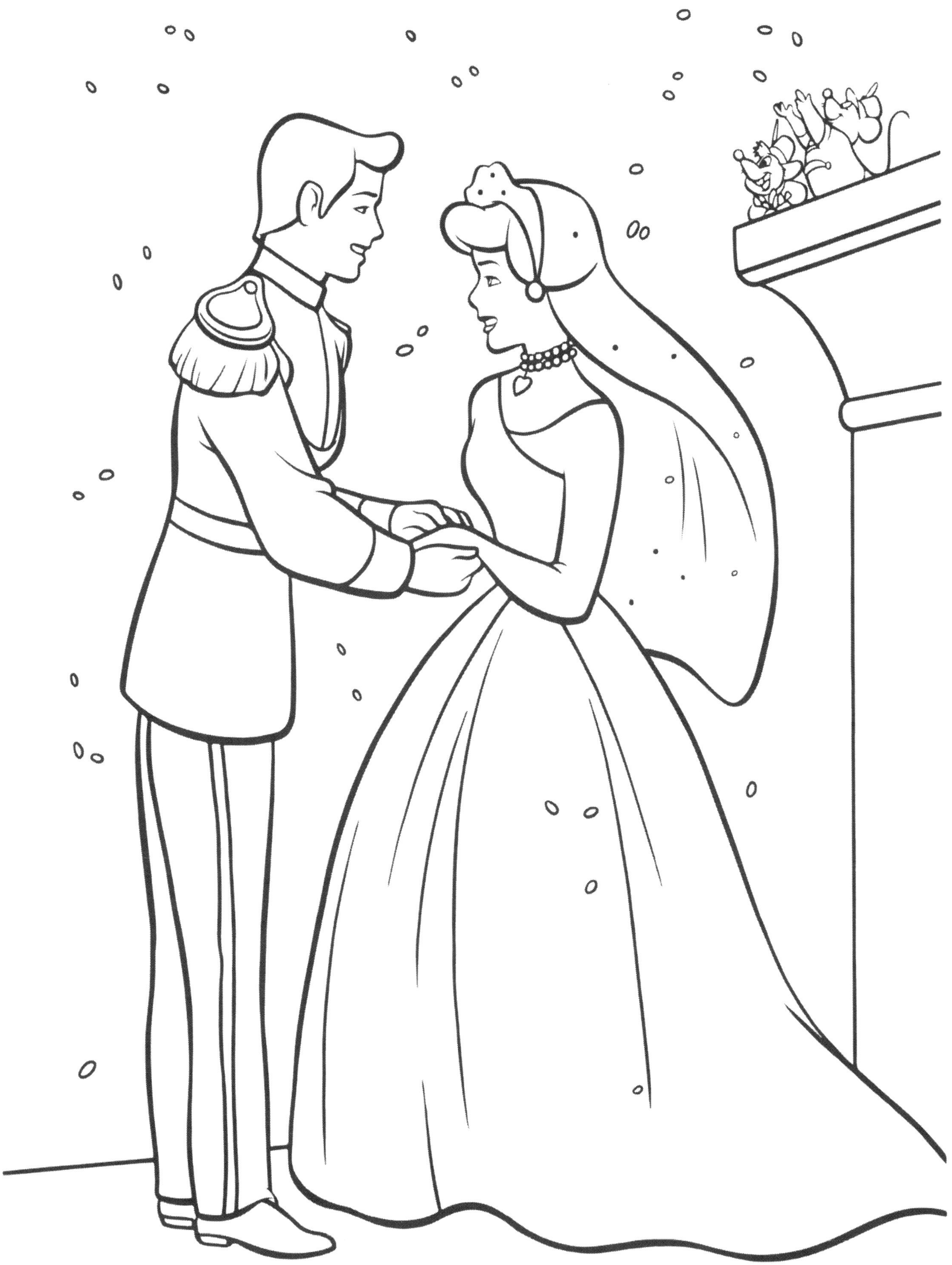

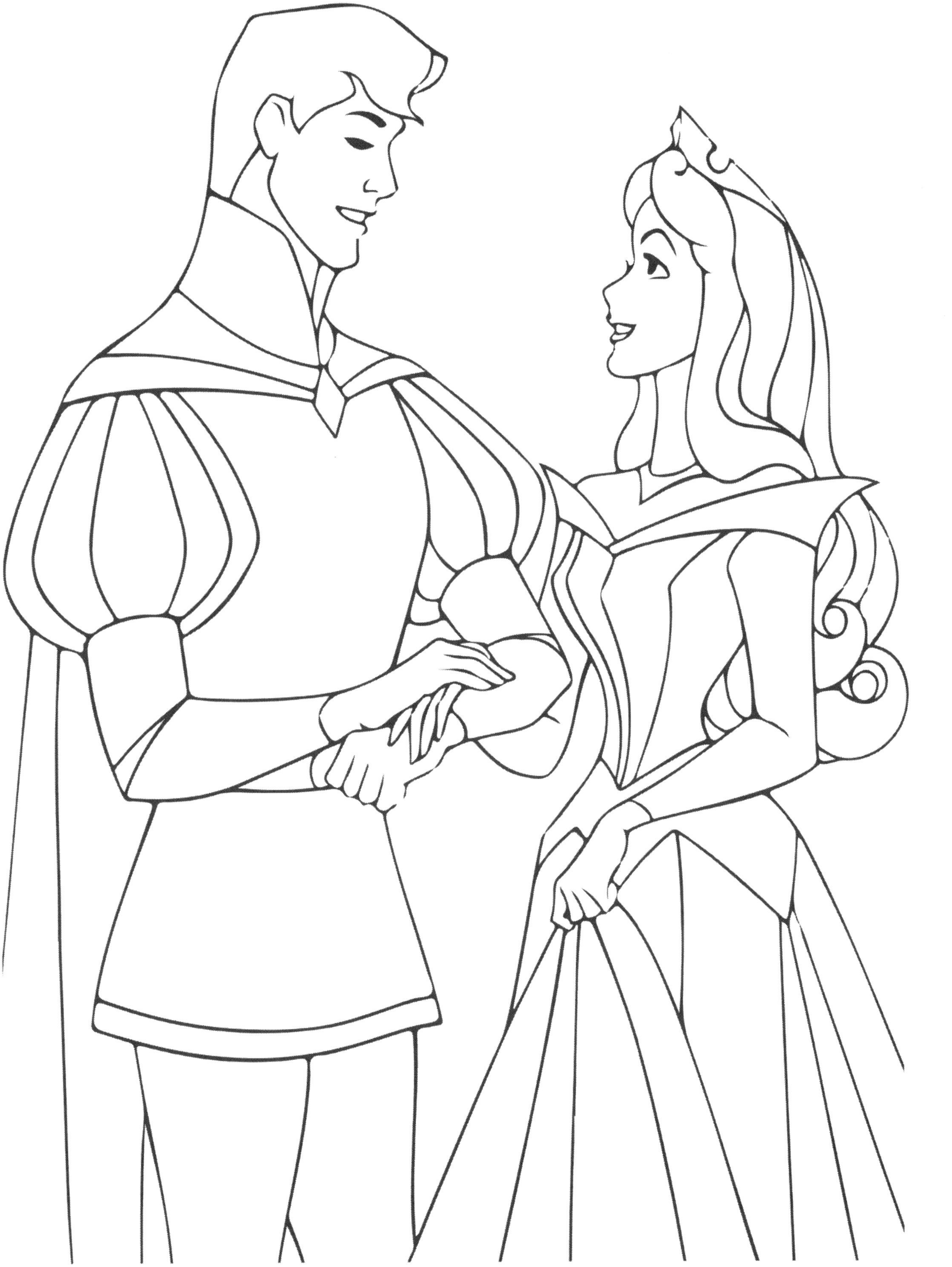

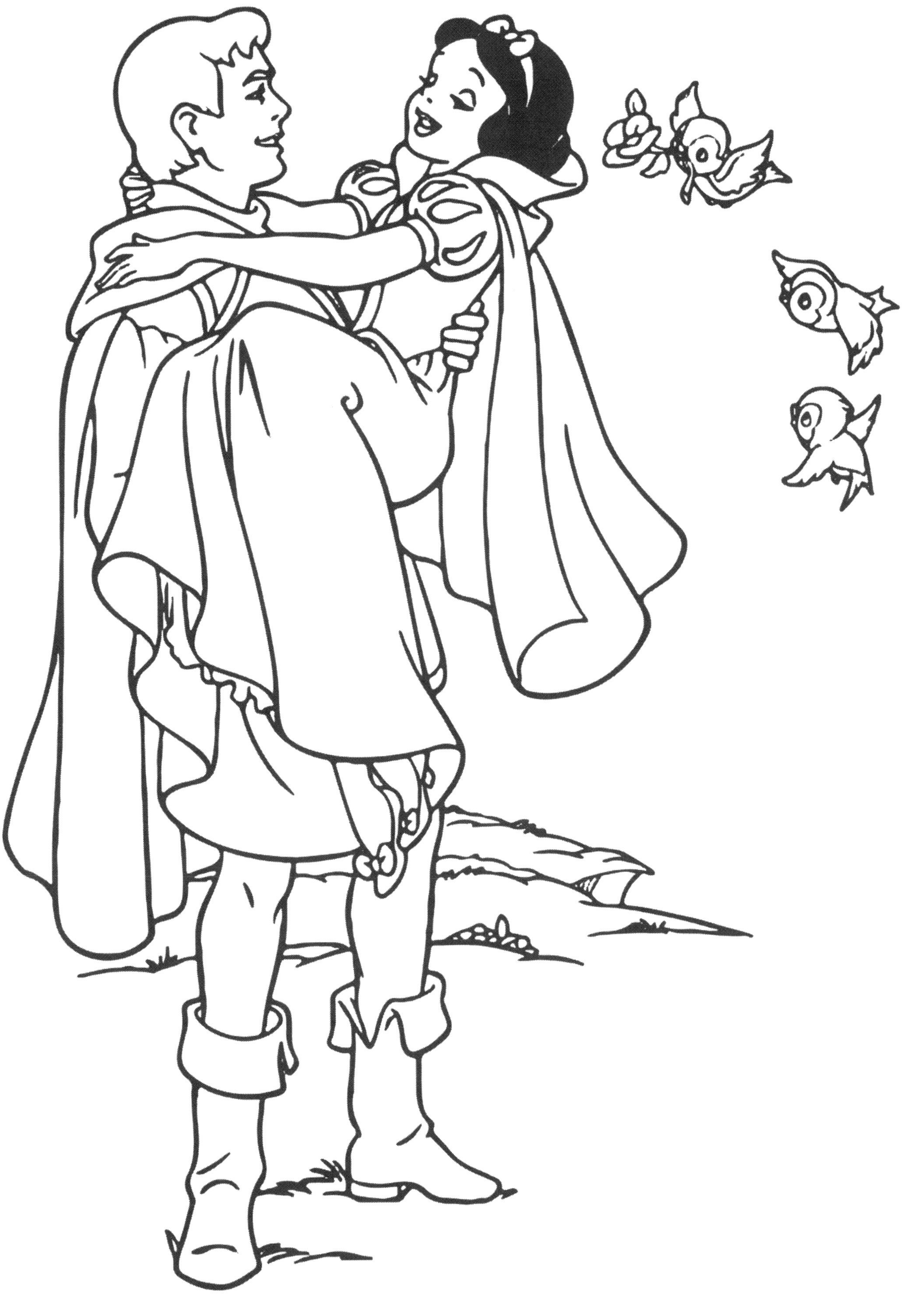

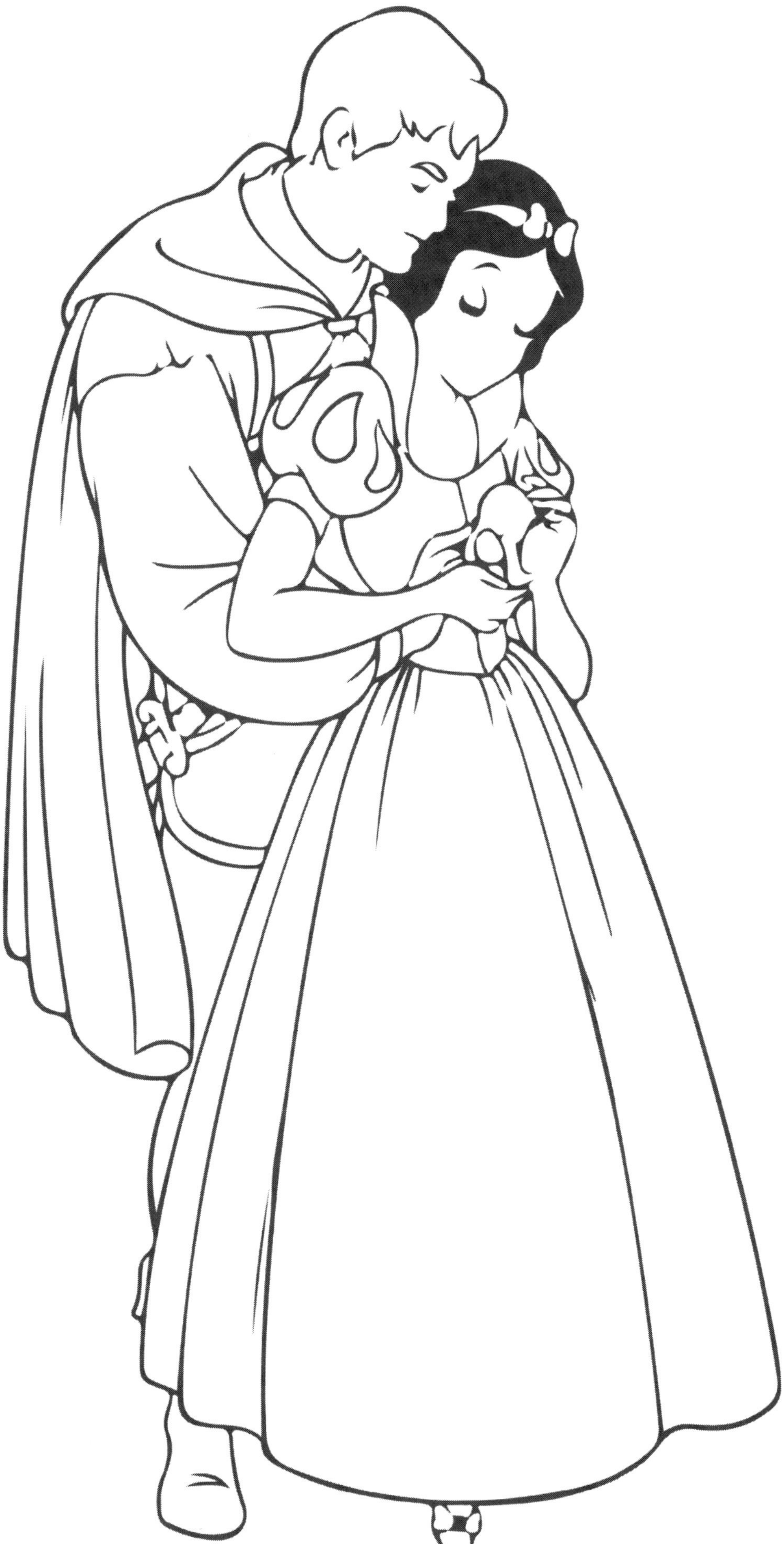

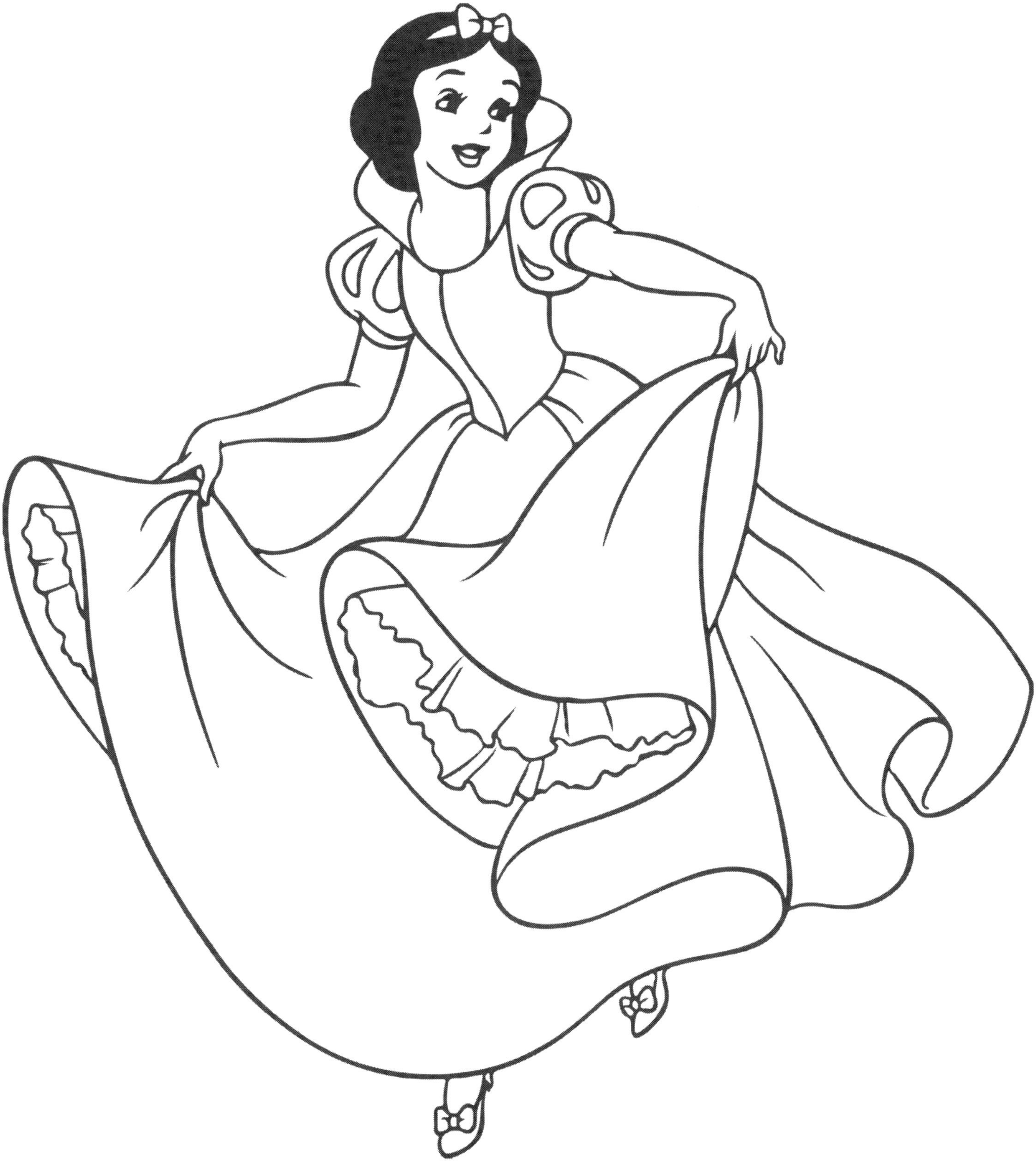

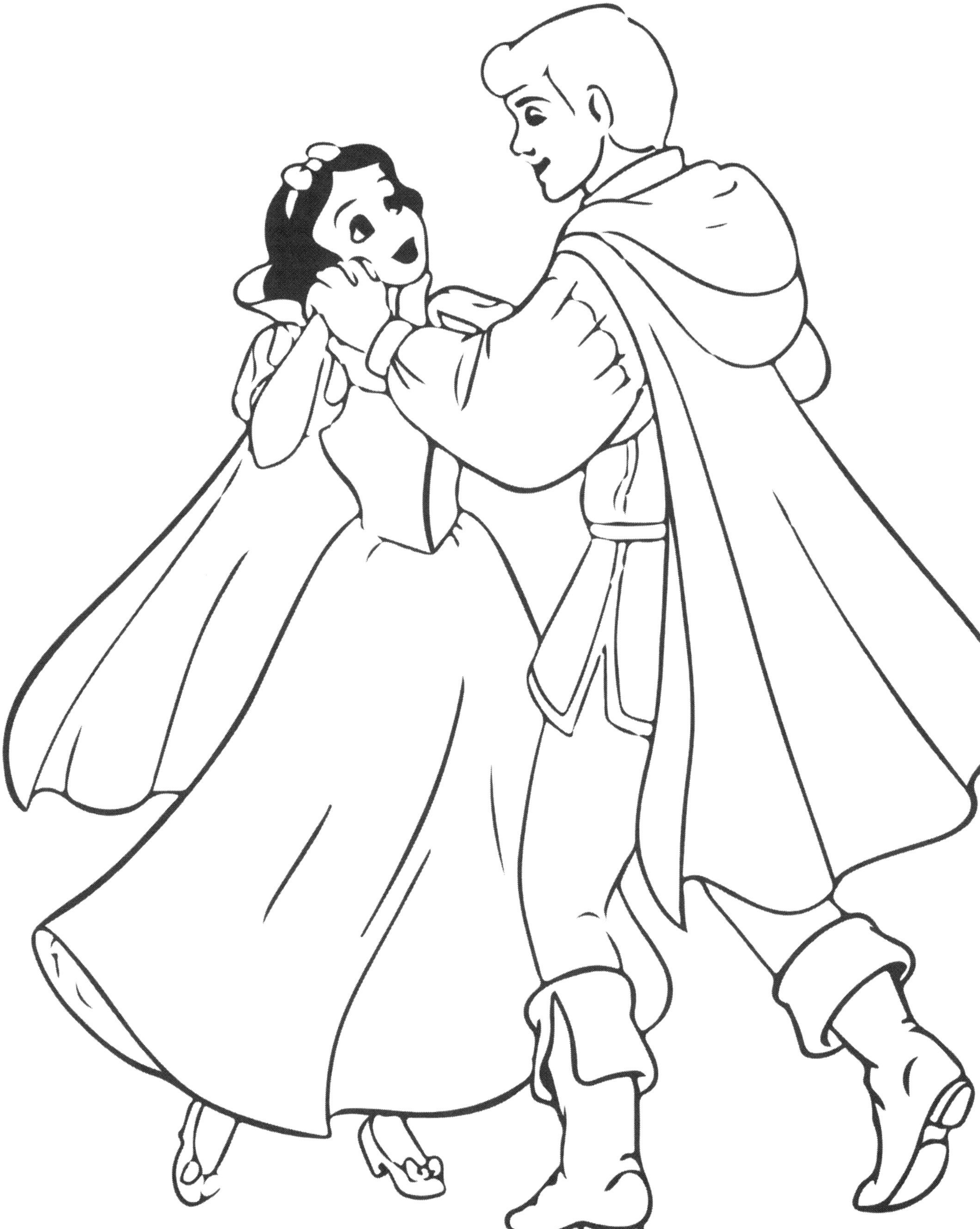

Made in United States
Orlando, FL
22 September 2022

22674063R00028